EASY COOKBOOK

THE EFFORTLESS CHEF SERIES

VOL. IX

By
Chef Maggie Chow
Copyright © 2015 by Saxonberg Associates
All rights reserved

Published by
BookSumo, a division of Saxonberg Associates
http://www.booksumo.com/

A Gift From Me To You...

I know you like cultural food. But what about Japanese Sushi?

Join my private mailing list of readers and get a copy of *Infinite Sushi: A*

Complete Set of Sushi and Japanese Recipes by fellow BookSumo author Hashimoto Kazuma for FREE!

Sign Me Up!

Enjoy some of the best sushi available!

You will also receive updates about all my new books when they are free. So please show your support.

Also don't forget to like and subscribe on the social networks. I love meeting my readers. Links to all my profiles are below so please click and connect :)

Facebook

Twitter

INTRODUCTION

Welcome to *The Effortless Chef Series*! Thank you for taking the time to download the *Easy Mexican Cookbook*. Come take a journey with me into the delights of easy cooking. The point of this cookbook and all my cookbooks is to exemplify the effortless nature of cooking simply.

In this book we focus on food from the Country of Mexico. You will find that even though the recipes are simple, the taste of the dishes is quite amazing.

So will you join me in an adventure of simple cooking? If the answer is yes (and I hope it is) please consult the table of contents to find the dishes you are most interested in. Once you are ready jump right in and start cooking.

— Chef Maggie Chow

Table of Contents

A Gift From Me To You... 2

Introduction 4

Table of Contents 5

Notice to Print Readers: 9

Legal Notes 10

   Breakfast Tacos From Mexico 11

   Green Chili Stew 14

   Ground Turkey Tacos 17

   Zucchini Enchiladas 20

   Mayan Couscous 23

   Calabacitas Guisada 26

   (Stewed Mexican Zucchini) 26

   Arroz Rojo 29

   (Mexican Red Rice) 29

   Biscochitos 32

   (Classical Mexcian Cookies) 32

Catalina's Mexican Rice 35

Salsa Verde 38

(Green Salsa from Morelos) 38

Mango Salsa Steak Fajitas............... 41

Migas 44

Mango Quesadillas........................... 47

Lengua 50

(Beef Tongue) 50

Sausage and Pepper Burrito............ 53

Quinoa Tacos 55

(Vegan Approved) 55

Sopes.. 58

(Mexican Fried Corn Snack) 58

Mexican Chili 60

Refried Bean Roll-Up....................... 63

Cheesy Poblano Chicken Enchiladas 65

Salads, Seasonings, Drinks, and Simple Mexican Side Dishes........................... 68

Taco Seasoning I 68

Refried Beans................................... 71

Mexican Rice.................................... 73

Taco Seasoning II 76
Elote 78
(Corn on the Cob Mexican Street Food) 78
Classic Margaritas In Mexico 81
Agua Fresca 84
(Mexican Watermelon Based Drink) 84
Horchata I 86
(Classical Spanish Milk Based Drink) 86
Horchata II 89
(Coconut Based) 89
Mexican-Style Hot Chocolate 92
Maria's Favorite Drink 95
(Honeydew Juice) 95
Berry Margaritas 97
Mandarin Margaritas 99
Mayan Mocha Powder 101
Licuado de Mango 103
Atole 105
(Spanish Hot Corn Drink) 105

Classical Sangrita 107

Mexican Style Ceviche 109

Mexican Green Papaya Salad 111

Enchilada Sauce 114

A Gift From Me To You 117

Come On... 119

Let's Be Friends :) 119

About The Publisher. 120

Can I Ask A Favour? 121

Interested in Other Easy Cookbooks? 122

NOTICE TO PRINT READERS:

Hey, because you purchased the print version of this book you are entitled to its original digital version for free by Amazon.

So when you have the time, please review your purchases, and download the Kindle version of this book.

You might enjoy consuming this book more in its original digital format.

;)

But, in any case, take care and enjoy reading in whatever format you choose!

LEGAL NOTES

ALL RIGHTS RESERVED. NO PART OF THIS BOOK MAY BE REPRODUCED OR TRANSMITTED IN ANY FORM OR BY ANY MEANS. PHOTOCOPYING, POSTING ONLINE, AND / OR DIGITAL COPYING IS STRICTLY PROHIBITED UNLESS WRITTEN PERMISSION IS GRANTED BY THE BOOK'S PUBLISHING COMPANY. LIMITED USE OF THE BOOK'S TEXT IS PERMITTED FOR USE IN REVIEWS WRITTEN FOR THE PUBLIC AND/OR PUBLIC DOMAIN.

Breakfast Tacos From Mexico

Ingredients:

- 6 oz. chorizo sausage
- 8 (6 inch) corn tortillas
- 6 eggs
- 1/4 cup milk
- 1/2 tsp pepper
- 1/2 tsp salt
- 1 cup shredded Monterey Jack cheese
- 1 dash hot pepper sauce (e.g. Tabasco™), or to taste
- 1/2 cup salsa

Directions:

- Cook crumbled sausage in a pan at medium heat until golden brown in color.
- Heat up two different pans at high heat and medium heat.

- Whisk together eggs, pepper and salt in a bowl, and pour these eggs into the pan at medium heat.
- Cook until you see that the eggs are firm and continue cooking after adding sausage.
- Warm up some tortillas in the pan which is at high heat for about 45 seconds each side and add some cheese before filling with the egg and tortilla mixture you have prepared.
- Also add some hot pepper sauce and salsa according to your taste before serving it.
- Enjoy.

Serving: 4

Timing Information:

Preparation	Cooking	Total Time
5 min	10 min	15 min

Nutritional Information:

Calories	537 kcal
Carbohydrates	27.7 g
Cholesterol	343 mg
Fat	34.1 g
Fiber	3.9 g
Protein	30.6 g
Sodium	1298 mg

* Percent Daily Values are based on a 2,000 calorie diet.

Green Chili Stew

Ingredients:

- 1 tbsp vegetable oil
- 2 pounds cubed beef stew meat
- 1 onion, chopped
- 1 (10 oz.) can diced tomatoes with green chili peppers
- 1 1/2 cups beef broth
- 1 (4 oz.) can chopped green chili peppers
- 1 tsp garlic salt
- 1 tsp ground cumin
- salt to taste
- ground black pepper to taste
- 2 large potatoes, peeled and cubed

Directions:

- Cook stew meat and onions in hot oil for about 5 minutes or until the onions are tender.
- Now add diced tomatoes with chilies, beef broth, salt, chili peppers, pepper, garlic salt and cumin.

- Bring to a boil and cook for one hour after turning the heat to low, while adding water or more beef if needed during this time.
- Now add potatoes into this mixture and cook for another 30 minutes or until you see that the potatoes are tender.
- Serve.

Serving: 4

Timing Information:

Preparation	Cooking	Total Time
15 min	1 hr 15 min	1 hr 30 min

Nutritional Information:

Calories	549 kcal
Carbohydrates	33 g
Cholesterol	122 mg
Fat	26.5 g
Fiber	3.3 g
Protein	43.6 g
Sodium	1455 mg

* Percent Daily Values are based on a 2,000 calorie diet.

Ground Turkey Tacos

Ingredients:

Tacos:

- 1 tbsp vegetable oil
- 1 pound lean (at least 93%) ground turkey
- 1 (1 oz.) package taco seasoning mix
- 2/3 cup water
- 1 (4.6 oz.) package taco shells

Toppings:

- 2 medium avocados, pitted, peeled and sliced
- 1 cup sliced pineapple (fresh or canned)

Directions:

- Cook turkey in hot oil over medium heat in a large skillet until you see that it is no longer pink.

- Drain any water and add taco seasoning mix and some water before turning the heat down and cooking it for another 10 minutes or until you find that the sauce is getting thick.
- Put this into taco shells.
- Serve.

Serving: 8

Timing Information:

Preparation	Cooking	Total Time
10 min		20 min

Nutritional Information:

Calories	549 kcal
Carbohydrates	39.1 g
Cholesterol	84 mg
Fat	33.8 g
Fiber	8.3 g
Protein	26.7 g
Sodium	872 mg

* Percent Daily Values are based on a 2,000 calorie diet.

Zucchini Enchiladas

Ingredients:

- 2 tbsps butter
- 1 1/2 pounds sliced zucchini
- 1 pound mushrooms, sliced
- 1 onion, sliced
- 1 1/2 pounds tomatoes, chopped
- salt and pepper to taste
- 1 1/2 pounds Monterey Jack cheese, shredded
- 10 (10 inch) flour tortillas

Directions:

- Preheat your oven to 350 degrees F and put some oil on a baking dish before doing anything else.
- Cook zucchini, onion, tomatoes, mushrooms, salt and pepper in hot oil butter over medium heat until the vegetables are tender.
- Place tortillas in the preheated oven for about 3 minutes to get them warm before folding them around the zucchini mixture and Monterey jack cheese, while saving some both for further use.

- Place these tortillas in the baking dish and cover them with the remaining zucchini mixture, while topping with cheese.
- Now bake this in the preheated oven for about 15 minutes or until the cheese starts to form bubbles.
- Enjoy.

Serving: 10

Timing Information:

Preparation	Cooking	Total Time
15 min	30 min	45 min

Nutritional Information:

Calories	537 kcal
Carbohydrates	44.9 g
Cholesterol	67 mg
Fat	28.9 g
Fiber	4.4 g
Protein	25.6 g
Sodium	852 mg

* Percent Daily Values are based on a 2,000 calorie diet.

Mayan Couscous

Ingredients:

- 1 cup couscous
- 1/2 tsp ground cumin
- 1 tsp salt, or to taste
- 1 1/4 cups boiling water
- 1 clove unpeeled garlic
- 1 (15 oz.) can black beans, rinsed and drained
- 1 cup canned whole kernel corn, drained
- 1/2 cup finely chopped red onion
- 1/4 cup chopped fresh cilantro
- 1 jalapeno pepper, minced
- 3 tbsps olive oil
- 3 tbsps fresh lime juice, or to taste

Directions:

- Add boiling water into a mixture of salt and couscous in a large sized bowl, and cover it with plastic wrap before letting it stand for about ten minutes.

- In this time, cook unpeeled garlic in hot oil over medium heat until it has turned golden brown.
- Now mash this garlic and add it into the couscous along with black beans, onion, cilantro, corn, jalapeno pepper, olive oil, and lime juice.
- Serve.

Serving: 15

Timing Information:

Preparation	Cooking	Total Time
15 min		25 min

Nutritional Information:

Calories	300 kcal
Carbohydrates	44.8 g
Cholesterol	0 mg
Fat	10.9 g
Fiber	3.6 g
Protein	7.1 g
Sodium	713 mg

* Percent Daily Values are based on a 2,000 calorie diet.

CALABACITAS GUISADA

(STEWED MEXICAN ZUCCHINI)

Ingredients:

- 1 tbsp vegetable oil
- 1/2 small white onion, sliced thinly
- 2 cloves garlic, minced
- 4 zucchini, sliced 1/4-inch thick
- 1 (14 oz.) can stewed tomatoes
- salt to taste
- 1 cup shredded mild Cheddar cheese

Directions:

- Cook onion and garlic in hot oil at medium heat in a pan for about 5 minutes or until soft.
- Mix gently after adding stewed tomatoes and zucchini.
- Cover the pan with a lid and cook for about 10 minutes or until the zucchini is tender.
- Add salt according to your taste and also some cheese.

- Let it stand as it is until the cheese has melted completely.
- Serve and enjoy.

Serving: 8

Timing Information:

Preparation	Cooking	Total Time
10 min	15 min	25 min

Nutritional Information:

Calories	97 kcal
Carbohydrates	5.8 g
Cholesterol	15 mg
Fat	6.6 g
Fiber	1.2 g
Protein	4.8 g
Sodium	202 mg

* Percent Daily Values are based on a 2,000 calorie diet.

Arroz Rojo

(Mexican Red Rice)

Ingredients:

- 2 Roma (plum tomatoes), cored
- 2 tbsps vegetable oil
- 1 cup minced onion
- 2 cloves garlic, minced
- 1 cup uncooked long-grain white rice
- 1 3/4 cups low-sodium chicken broth
- 1/4 cup canned tomato sauce
- 1 jalapeno pepper, chopped
- 2 sprigs fresh cilantro
- salt to taste

Directions:

- Using a box grater and discarding the skin of tomatoes, grate the tomatoes and put them in a medium sized bowl.
- Now cook onion and add garlic in hot oil for about 5 minutes before

garlic and one minute after adding garlic.
- Now add rice and cook for another 3 minutes to get rice slightly toasted.
- Bring everything to a boil after adding chicken tomato sauce, grated tomato, and chicken broth.
- Sprinkle jalapeno pepper, salt, and cilantro before turning the heat down to low and cooking for another 15 minutes while keeping the lid on the skillet.
- Now remove the rice from the heat and let it stand covered in the skillet for about 8 minutes before transferring to the serving dish.

Serving: 5

Timing Information:

Preparation	Cooking	Total Time
15 min	25 min	40 min

Nutritional Information:

Calories	213 kcal
Carbohydrates	35.1 g
Cholesterol	1 mg
Fat	6 g
Fiber	1.6 g
Protein	4.6 g
Sodium	109 mg

* Percent Daily Values are based on a 2,000 calorie diet.

BISCOCHITOS

(CLASSICAL MEXCIAN COOKIES)

Ingredients:

- 6 cups all-purpose flour
- 1 tbsp baking powder
- 1/4 tsp salt
- 2 cups lard
- 1 1/2 cups white sugar
- 2 tsps anise seed
- 2 eggs
- 1/4 cup brandy
- 1/4 cup white sugar
- 1 tbsp ground cinnamon

Directions:

- Preheat your oven to 400 degrees F and combine flour, salt and baking powder in a bowl before doing anything else.
- Whisk lard and a half cup of sugar very thoroughly before adding anise seed and whisking it again until smooth.

- Add eggs one by one into this mixture and also add the flour mixture.
- Now roll this dough on a floured surface to a thickness of half an inch and cut it into shapes of your own choice.
- Sprinkle mixture of sugar and cinnamon over it in the baking sheets and bake this in the preheated oven for about 10 minutes or until lightly brown.

Serving: 6

Timing Information:

Preparation	Cooking	Total Time
15 min	10 min	25 min

Nutritional Information:

Calories	113 kcal
Carbohydrates	13 g
Cholesterol	11 mg
Fat	5.9 g
Fiber	0.3 g
Protein	1.3 g
Sodium	24 mg

* Percent Daily Values are based on a 2,000 calorie diet.

Catalina's Mexican Rice

Ingredients:

- 2 tbsps olive oil
- 1 cup rice
- 1/2 large onion, diced
- 1/2 tbsp salt
- 1/8 tsp ground cumin
- 1/8 tsp ground black pepper
- 2 1/2 cups water
- 1/3 cup tomato sauce
- 1 tbsp chicken bouillon
- 1 whole serrano chili pepper (optional)

Directions:

- Cook onion and rice in hot oil at medium heat for about 5 minutes or until golden brown and add pepper, salt and cumin.
- Now pour in some water over this mixture before adding chicken bouillon and tomato sauce.
- Bring this to a boil over medium heat after covering.

- Now add some chili pepper and cook for another 10 minutes.
- Now turn the heat down to low and cook for another 20 minutes.
- Let cool. Serve and enjoy.

Serving: 6

Timing Information:

Preparation	Cooking	Total Time
10 min	30 min	40 min

Nutritional Information:

Calories	164 kcal
Carbohydrates	26.8 g
Cholesterol	1 mg
Fat	4.9 g
Fiber	0.9 g
Protein	2.7 g
Sodium	845 mg

* Percent Daily Values are based on a 2,000 calorie diet.

SALSA VERDE

(GREEN SALSA FROM MORELOS)

Ingredients:

- 2 pounds tomatillos, husked
- 2 fresh jalapeno peppers
- 3 cloves garlic, peeled
- 1 dash cloves
- 1/2 tsp ground cumin
- 1 dash black pepper
- 1 tsp chicken bouillon granules, or salt

Directions:

- Cook tomatillos, jalapenos and garlic in a large sized pan after putting in water.
- Now bring this to a boil and cook for about 10 minutes or until the color of the tomatillos turn yellow after turning down the heat to medium.

- Allow it to cool down for 10 minutes and after removing all the water from; put these tomatillos, along with cloves, pepper, cumin and chicken bouillon into the blender.
- Blend until the required smoothness is achieved.
- Serve.

Serving: 1 quart

Timing Information:

Preparation	Cooking	Total Time
10 min	10 min	30 min

Nutritional Information:

Calories	20 kcal
Carbohydrates	3.7 g
Cholesterol	< 1 mg
Fat	0.6 g
Fiber	1.2 g
Protein	0.6 g
Sodium	24 mg

* Percent Daily Values are based on a 2,000 calorie diet.

Mango Salsa Steak Fajitas

Ingredients:

Tacos:

- 1 tbsp vegetable oil
- 1 (1 oz.) package taco seasoning mix
- 1 (1 1/4 pound) flank steak, trimmed of excess fat
- 8 (6 inch) flour tortillas for soft tacos & fajitas
- Mango Salsa:
- 2 ripe medium mangoes, seed removed, peeled and diced
- Juice of 1 medium lime
- 1 jalapeno chili, seeded, chopped
- 1/4 cup chopped red onion
- 1/4 cup chopped fresh cilantro leaves

Directions:

- Preheat your oven to 400 degrees F before doing anything else.
- Cook flank steak after putting taco seasoning and mix over it on

high heat until golden brown and place this in the preheated oven until tender.
- Let it cool down for about 10 minutes and in this time, combine all the salsa ingredients thoroughly.
- Cut down the prepared steak into small pieces and fold tortillas in three pieces with some salsa.
- Serve.

Serving: 8

Timing Information:

Preparation	Cooking	Total Time
15 min	30 min	45 min

Nutritional Information:

Calories	391 kcal
Carbohydrates	46.5 g
Cholesterol	31 mg
Fat	13.9 g
Fiber	3.2 g
Protein	21.6 g
Sodium	1068 mg

* Percent Daily Values are based on a 2,000 calorie diet.

Migas

Ingredients:

- 1 tbsp butter
- 1 (4 oz.) can chopped green chilis
- 1/2 tomato, chopped
- 6 large eggs
- 1/4 cup crushed tortilla chips, or to taste
- 1/4 cup shredded sharp Cheddar cheese
- 6 (8 inch) flour tortillas
- 6 tbsps taco sauce (enchilada sauce), to taste (optional)

Directions:

- Cook tomato and green chili in hot oil butter for about five minutes before adding eggs and cooking for another 3 minutes.
- Now add some tortilla chips over the eggs and mix well before turning off the heat and adding cheese.

- Now cover the pan and let the cheese melt down and the eggs get tender.
- Get tortillas warm in a microwave for about 30 seconds and fold them around the egg mixture you just prepared.
- Put some taco sauce over it before serving.
- Enjoy.

Serving: 6

Timing Information:

Preparation	Cooking	Total Time
10 min	10 min	20 min

Nutritional Information:

Calories	283 kcal
Carbohydrates	30.8 g
Cholesterol	196 mg
Fat	12.2 g
Fiber	2 g
Protein	12.1 g
Sodium	661 mg

* Percent Daily Values are based on a 2,000 calorie diet.

Mango Quesadillas

Ingredients:

- 1 (15 oz.) can black beans, drained
- 1 tbsp vegetable oil
- 1/2 onion, chopped
- 1 red bell pepper, chopped
- 1 tsp chili powder
- 1 pinch cayenne pepper
- 1 pinch dried oregano
- 1 pinch dried basil
- 1 mango - peeled, seeded and diced
- 1 (6 oz.) package seasoned chicken-style vegetarian strips (such as Lightlife Smart Strips)
- 6 (10 inch) flour tortillas
- 1 (8 oz.) package shredded Cheddar cheese
- 1 cup arugula leaves
- 1 (4 oz.) jar jalapeno pepper rings (optional)
- 1 (8 oz.) jar salsa

Directions:

- Cook beans for 5 minutes at medium heat, mash them and after turning the heat down to low, cook for few more minutes.
- Now cook onion and red bell pepper in hot oil until the vegetables are tender, while adding basil, cayenne pepper and oregano for taste.
- Also add vegetarian chicken strips and mango, and cook for another 2 minutes or until the chicken strips are tender.
- Cook tortillas in a pan for about 2 minutes on each side before filling with black beans, cheddar, jalapenos, mango mixture and arugula, and folding it up.
- Serve with salsa.

Serving: 6

Timing Information:

Preparation	Cooking	Total Time
10 min	20 min	30 min

Nutritional Information:

Calories	503 kcal
Carbohydrates	49.2 g
Cholesterol	39 mg
Fat	24.2 g
Fiber	5.8 g
Protein	23.2 g
Sodium	1421 mg

* Percent Daily Values are based on a 2,000 calorie diet.

Lengua

(Beef Tongue)

Ingredients:

- 1 beef tongue
- 1/2 onion
- 2 cloves garlic, or more to taste
- 1 bay leaf
- salt and ground black pepper to taste
- water to cover
- 1 tbsp butter

Directions:

- Cook beef tongue, garlic and onion in slow cooker after pouring in enough water to cover the meat plus a bit more for about 8 hours and let it cool down.
- Remove the outer surface of the beef tongue and cut it into small pieces.
- Now cook these small pieces of beef tongue in hot oil and butter

in a pan at medium heat for about 10 minutes.
- Add some salt and pepper according to your taste before serving with rice.
- Enjoy.

Serving: 6

Timing Information:

Preparation	Cooking	Total Time
15 min	8 hr 5 min	8 hr 20 min

Nutritional Information:

Calories	492 kcal
Carbohydrates	1.2 g
Cholesterol	224 mg
Fat	38.8 g
Fiber	0.2 g
Protein	32.1 g
Sodium	123 mg

* Percent Daily Values are based on a 2,000 calorie diet.

Sausage and Pepper Burrito

Ingredients:

- 4 links breakfast pork sausage, cut into 1/2-inch pieces
- 1/2 red onion, sliced
- 1/2 cup red pepper strips
- 1/2 cup green pepper strips
- 4 eggs, beaten
- 4 (8 inch) whole wheat tortillas
- 1 cup shred cheddar cheese (extra sharp)

Directions:

- Cook peppers, sausage and onion in a pan over medium heat for about 5 minutes.
- Now cook eggs in a pan for 2 minutes and add sausage mixture over it, while topping with cheese.
- Fold tortillas around this mixture and serve.
- Enjoy.

Serving: 4

Timing Information:

Preparation	Cooking	Total Time
15 min		15 min

Nutritional Information:

Calories	341 kcal
Carbohydrates	30.2 g
Cholesterol	235 mg
Fat	19.6 g
Fiber	3.1 g
Protein	20.4 g
Sodium	582 mg

* Percent Daily Values are based on a 2,000 calorie diet.

Quinoa Tacos

(Vegan Approved)

Ingredients:

- 1 tsp olive oil
- 1 onion, chopped
- 2 (8 oz.) cans tomato sauce
- 1 1/2 cups water
- 1/2 cup quinoa
- 1 (1 oz.) envelope taco seasoning mix
- 2 (14.5 oz.) cans black beans, rinsed and drained
- 24 corn tortillas

Directions:

- Cook onion in hot oil for about 10 minutes before adding tomato sauce, taco seasoning, water and quinoa, and bring this mixture to a boil.
- Turn the heat down and cook for 15 minutes before adding black beans and cooking for another 5 minutes.

- Fill tortillas with this mixture and serve.

Serving: 8

Timing Information:

Preparation	Cooking	Total Time
15 min	25 min	40 min

Nutritional Information:

Calories	339 kcal
Carbohydrates	65.4 g
Cholesterol	0 mg
Fat	3.9 g
Fiber	13.8 g
Protein	13 g
Sodium	985 mg

* Percent Daily Values are based on a 2,000 calorie diet.

Sopes

(Mexican Fried Corn Snack)

Ingredients:

- 3 cups masa harina
- 1 tbsp salt
- 2 cups warm water, or as needed
- 1 quart oil for frying

Directions:

- Combine masa harina and salt together while adding water until you have smooth dough.
- Make 2 inch balls and flatten it out.
- Now fry this dough in hot oil for about 30 seconds on each side until brown.
- Let it cool after placing on a paper towel and now pinch the edges of every ball.
- Now fry it again in the hot oil until golden brown, which will take about another 2 minutes.

Serving: 12

Timing Information:

Preparation	Cooking	Total Time
15 min	10 min	25 min

Nutritional Information:

Calories	169 kcal
Carbohydrates	21.7 g
Cholesterol	0 mg
Fat	8.4 g
Fiber	3.8 g
Protein	2.7 g
Sodium	584 mg

* Percent Daily Values are based on a 2,000 calorie diet.

MEXICAN CHILI

Ingredients:

- 2 tbsps vegetable oil
- 1 1/2 pounds cubed pork stew meat
- 2 tbsps all-purpose flour
- 1 (4.5 oz.) can diced green chili peppers, drained
- 1/2 (3.5 oz.) can chopped jalapeno peppers
- 1/2 medium onion, chopped
- 5 tbsps tomato sauce
- 3 1/2 cups water
- onion salt to taste
- garlic salt to taste
- salt and black pepper to taste

Directions:

- Cook cubed pork in hot oil over medium heat in a pan for about 15 minutes and allow it to cool down.
- Now add flour over the pork and Mix well before adding tomato sauce, chili peppers, jalapenos,

onion salt, pepper, garlic salt, and pure salt into.
- Mix well and cook after covering the pan for about 30 minutes while stirring at constant time intervals.
- Now remove the cover from the pan and cook it for another 10 minutes.
- Serve.

Serving: 6

Timing Information:

Preparation	Cooking	Total Time
15 min	1 hr	1 hr 15 min

Nutritional Information:

Calories	339 kcal
Carbohydrates	65.4 g
Cholesterol	0 mg
Fat	3.9 g
Fiber	13.8 g
Protein	13 g
Sodium	985 mg

* Percent Daily Values are based on a 2,000 calorie diet.

Refried Bean Roll-Up

Ingredients:

- 1 (16 oz.) can fat-free refried beans
- 1/2 cup Thick 'n Chunky salsa
- 1/2 tsp chili powder
- 8 fat free flour tortillas (8 to10 inch)
- 1 cup shredded lettuce
- 1/2 cup shredded Monterey Jack cheese

Directions:

- Cook salsa, chili powder and beans over medium heat for about 5 minutes.
- Now roll tortillas around this mixture after putting lettuce and cheese over it.
- Serve this with salsa if you like.
- Enjoy.

Serving: 8

Timing Information:

Preparation	Cooking	Total Time
10 min		15 min

Nutritional Information:

Calories	547 kcal
Carbohydrates	86.8 g
Cholesterol	13 mg
Fat	4.4 g
Fiber	9.7 g
Protein	19.5 g
Sodium	1414 mg

* Percent Daily Values are based on a 2,000 calorie diet.

Cheesy Poblano Chicken Enchiladas

Ingredients:

- 2 cups shredded cooked chicken
- 1 (10.75 oz.) can Poblano Soup
- 1/4 cup salsa
- 1/2 cup shredded Monterey Jack cheese or crumbled queso fresco (preferred)
- 1/4 cup milk
- 6 (6 inch) corn tortillas, warmed
- 1/2 cup chopped tomato
- 2 tbsps sliced green onions
- 1 tbsp chopped fresh cilantro leaves

Directions:

- Preheat your oven to 400 degrees F before doing anything else.
- Now combine half cup soup, cheese and salsa in a medium sized bowl, and roll up tortillas around this mixture.

- Now pour the mixture of the remaining soup and some milk over the filled tortillas before putting it into the preheated oven in a baking dish for 30 minutes.
- Serve.

Serving: 6

Timing Information:

Preparation	Cooking	Total Time
15 min	30 min	45 min

Nutritional Information:

Calories	233 kcal
Carbohydrates	17.4 g
Cholesterol	50 mg
Fat	10.3 g
Fiber	2.2 g
Protein	17.5 g
Sodium	541 mg

* Percent Daily Values are based on a 2,000 calorie diet.

Salads, Seasonings, Drinks, and Simple Mexican Side Dishes

Taco Seasoning I

Ingredients:

- 1 tbsp chili powder
- 1/4 tsp garlic powder
- 1/4 tsp onion powder
- 1/4 tsp crushed red pepper flakes
- 1/4 tsp dried oregano
- 1/2 tsp paprika
- 1 1/2 tsps ground cumin
- 1 tsp sea salt
- 1 tsp black pepper

Directions:

- Take out all the ingredients mentioned above and combine them thoroughly.

- Store in an airtight container.
- Use for aforementioned recipes.
- Enjoy.

Serving: 1 oz.

Timing Information:

Preparation	Cooking	Total Time
1 min		1 min

Nutritional Information:

Calories	5 kcal
Carbohydrates	0.9 g
Cholesterol	0 mg
Fat	0.2 g
Fiber	0.4 g
Protein	0.2 g
Sodium	185 mg

* Percent Daily Values are based on a 2,000 calorie diet.

Refried Beans

Ingredients:

- 1 onion, peeled and cut in half
- 3 cups dry pinto beans, rinsed
- 1/2 fresh jalapeno pepper, seeded and chopped
- 2 tbsps minced garlic
- 5 tsps salt
- 1 3/4 tsps fresh ground black pepper
- 1/8 tsp ground cumin, optional
- 9 cups water

Directions:

- Cook onion, jalapeno, garlic, rinsed beans, salt, pepper, and cumin after adding water on high heat in a slow cooker for about 8 hours.
- Now take out the beans and mash them with a potato masher before putting them into the liquid again and heating it again to get the required consistency.

Serving: 15

Timing Information:

Preparation	Cooking	Total Time
15 min	8 hr	8 hr 15 min

Nutritional Information:

Calories	139 kcal
Carbohydrates	25.4 g
Cholesterol	0 mg
Fat	0.5 g
Fiber	6.2 g
Protein	8.5 g
Sodium	785 mg

* Percent Daily Values are based on a 2,000 calorie diet.

Mexican Rice

Ingredients:

- 1 cup long grain white rice
- 1 tbsp vegetable oil
- 1 1/2 cups chicken broth
- 1/2 onion, finely chopped
- 1/2 green bell pepper, finely chopped
- 1 fresh jalapeno pepper, chopped
- 1 tomato, seeded and chopped
- 1 cube chicken bouillon
- salt and pepper to taste
- 1/2 tsp ground cumin
- 1/2 cup chopped fresh cilantro
- 1 clove garlic, cut in half

Directions:

- Cook rice in hot oil for about 3 minutes on medium heat in a pan before adding chicken broth and bringing it to a boil.
- Now add onion, diced tomato, green pepper, jalapeno, bouillon cube, salt and pepper, cumin, cilantro, and garlic.

- Bring this mixture to a boil and turn the heat down to low, and cook for another 20 minutes.
- Serve.

Serving: 5

Timing Information:

Preparation	Cooking	Total Time
5 min	25 min	30 min

Nutritional Information:

Calories	158 kcal
Carbohydrates	29.1 g
Cholesterol	1 mg
Fat	2.8 g
Fiber	1.1 g
Protein	3.4 g
Sodium	631 mg

* Percent Daily Values are based on a 2,000 calorie diet.

TACO SEASONING II

Ingredients:

- 1 tbsp cornstarch
- 2 tsps chili powder
- 1 tsp salt
- 1 tsp paprika
- 1 tsp white sugar
- 1/2 tsp onion powder
- 1/2 tsp garlic powder
- 1/4 tsp cayenne pepper
- 1/2 tsp ground cumin

Directions:

- Combine all the spices together in a bowl and store it in an airtight container.
- Use for any meat which you desire to have a Mexican style taste or for meat to be placed on the grill.
- Enjoy.

Serving: 3 tbsps

Timing Information:

Preparation	Cooking	Total Time
5 min		5 min

Nutritional Information:

Calories	21 kcal
Carbohydrates	4.6 g
Cholesterol	0 mg
Fat	0.4 g
Fiber	0.8 g
Protein	0.4 g
Sodium	596 mg

* Percent Daily Values are based on a 2,000 calorie diet.

ELOTE

(CORN ON THE COB MEXICAN STREET FOOD)

Ingredients:

- 4 ears corn, shucked
- 1/4 cup melted butter
- 1/4 cup mayonnaise
- 1/2 cup grated cotija cheese
- 4 wedges lime (optional)

Directions:

- First, preheat your grill for medium heat before starting anything else.
- Now take out the corn and grill it on the preheated grill for about 10 minutes or until lightly brown.
- Cook it in some melted butter and evenly spread mayonnaise over it.
- Also add some cojita cheese before serving for extra flavor.
- Enjoy.

NOTE: Grilled corn with mayo and cheese is very addicting.

Serving: 4

Timing Information:

Preparation	Cooking	Total Time
10 min	10 min	20 min

Nutritional Information:

Calories	386 kcal
Carbohydrates	28.9 g
Cholesterol	53 mg
Fat	29.1 g
Fiber	4 g
Protein	8.4 g
Sodium	368 mg

* Percent Daily Values are based on a 2,000 calorie diet.

CLASSIC MARGARITAS IN MEXICO

Ingredients:

- 5 fluid oz. tequila
- 3 fluid oz. fresh lime juice
- 1 fluid oz. sweetened lime juice
- 3 fluid oz. triple sec (orange-flavored liqueur)
- ice cubes
- 1 lime, cut into wedges
- rimming salt

Directions:

- Add tequila, lime juice, sweetened lime juice and triple sec in cocktail shaker before adding a scoop of ice cream
- Shake vigorously until you see that the shaker is frosty.
- Rub some lime wedge around the rim of margarita glass and add salt before putting in ice cubes into each glass.

- Some pour equal amount of cocktail you have prepared into each glass and serve.

Serving: 12 fluid oz.

Timing Information:

Preparation	Cooking	Total Time
5 min		5 min

Nutritional Information:

Calories	5 kcal
Carbohydrates	0.9 g
Cholesterol	0 mg
Fat	0.2 g
Fiber	0.4 g
Protein	0.2 g
Sodium	185 mg

* Percent Daily Values are based on a 2,000 calorie diet.

AGUA FRESCA

(MEXICAN WATERMELON BASED DRINK)

Ingredients:

- 4 cups cubed seeded watermelon
- 1/2 cup water
- 1/2 cup white sugar, or to taste
- 4 slices lime
- 24 fresh mint leaves
- ice

Directions:

- Add watermelon and some water into the blender and blend it until smooth before adding the sugar.
- Now cut lime slices in half and place each half in every glass along with mint leaves.
- Now fill each glass with ice cubes and pour in the blended watermelon.
- Stir it a bit before serving.
- Enjoy.

Serving: 8

Timing Information:

Preparation	Cooking	Total Time
25 min		25 min

Nutritional Information:

Calories	72 kcal
Carbohydrates	18.7 g
Cholesterol	0 mg
Fat	0.1 g
Fiber	0.4 g
Protein	0.5 g
Sodium	2 mg

* Percent Daily Values are based on a 2,000 calorie diet.

Horchata I

(Classical Spanish Milk Based Drink)

Ingredients:

- 1 cup uncooked white long-grain rice
- 5 cups water
- 1/2 cup milk
- 1/2 tbsp vanilla extract
- 1/2 tbsp ground cinnamon
- 2/3 cup white sugar

Directions:

- Blend rice and water in a food processor for about 1 minute and let it stand as it is for about three hours.
- Now take out all the water from it and in this water add milk, sugar, cinnamon and vanilla.
- Mix well and serve it in a glass over ice.

NOTE: This is a classical form of horchata other forms can be made with almonds, or barley, see next recipe for a tasty variation.

Serving: 10

Timing Information:

Preparation	Cooking	Total Time
10 min		3 hr 10 min

Nutritional Information:

Calories	213 kcal
Carbohydrates	48.4 g
Cholesterol	2 mg
Fat	0.6 g
Fiber	0.7 g
Protein	2.9 g
Sodium	16 mg

* Percent Daily Values are based on a 2,000 calorie diet.

Horchata II

(Coconut Based)

Ingredients:

- 1 cup uncooked white rice
- 1 cup almonds
- 1 cup sweetened flaked coconut
- 3 cups boiling water
- 1 (14 oz.) can coconut milk
- 1 (14 oz.) can sweetened condensed milk
- 5 cups cold water, or more as needed
- 5 cups ice

Directions:

- Blend rice, coconut flakes and almonds in a blender until really fine.
- Pour boiling water into this mixture and let it stand for at least 6 hours.
- Now take remove the water and add sweetened condensed milk and coconut milk to it.

- Pour this over ice cubes in a glass.
- Enjoy.

Serving: 12

Timing Information:

Preparation	Cooking	Total Time
15 min		6 hr 15 min

Nutritional Information:

Calories	322 kcal
Carbohydrates	36.5 g
Cholesterol	11 mg
Fat	17.6 g
Fiber	2.6 g
Protein	7.1 g
Sodium	72 mg

* Percent Daily Values are based on a 2,000 calorie diet.

Mexican-Style Hot Chocolate

Ingredients:

- 1 1/2 cups cold water
- 1/2 cup white sugar
- 1/4 cup unsweetened cocoa powder
- 2 tbsps all-purpose flour
- 1 tsp ground cinnamon
- 1/4 tsp ground cloves
- 1/4 tsp salt
- 6 cups whole milk
- 1 tbsp vanilla extract

Directions:

- Mix cold water, cocoa powder, sugar, flour, cinnamon, cloves, and salt in a pan very thoroughly before putting it over low heat and cooking it for about 4 minutes.
- Now add milk and cook for another two minutes before adding vanilla extract.

- Blend this in a food processor until the required smoothness is achieved.

Serving: 12

Timing Information:

Preparation	Cooking	Total Time
10 min	5 min	15 min

Nutritional Information:

Calories	118 kcal
Carbohydrates	16.1 g
Cholesterol	12 mg
Fat	4.2 g
Fiber	0.7 g
Protein	4.4 g
Sodium	99 mg

* Percent Daily Values are based on a 2,000 calorie diet.

Maria's Favorite Drink

(Honeydew Juice)

Ingredients:

- 1 (5 pound) honeydew melon, quartered and seeded
- 2 cups ice cubes
- 1 cup water
- 3 tbsps white sugar

Directions:

- Remove the flesh from the honeydew melon quarters and place into the blender along with ice cubes, sugar and water.
- Blend this until you see that the sugar has dissolved.
- Enjoy.

Serving: 6

Timing Information:

Preparation	Cooking	Total Time
10 min		10 min

Nutritional Information:

Calories	159 kcal
Carbohydrates	40.3 g
Cholesterol	0 mg
Fat	0.5 g
Fiber	3 g
Protein	2 g
Sodium	71 mg

* Percent Daily Values are based on a 2,000 calorie diet.

Berry Margaritas

Ingredients:

- 3 cups ice
- 1 cup tequila
- 2/3 cup triple sec
- 1/2 cup orange juice
- 2/3 cup frozen strawberries
- 2/3 cup frozen blueberries
- 2/3 cup frozen raspberries
- 3 tbsps white sugar

Directions:

- Put tequila, orange juice, strawberries, triple sec, blueberries, raspberries, and sugar in a blender, and blend it until the required smoothness is achieved.
- Pour this into glasses of your choice and serve.
- Enjoy.

Serving: 6

Timing Information:

Preparation	Cooking	Total Time
10 min		10 min

Nutritional Information:

Calories	245 kcal
Carbohydrates	26.6 g
Cholesterol	0 mg
Fat	0.3 g
Fiber	1.4 g
Protein	0.5 g
Sodium	7 mg

* Percent Daily Values are based on a 2,000 calorie diet.

Mandarin Margaritas

Ingredients:

- 1 cup fresh tangerine juice
- 1 cup ice
- 2 (1.5 fluid oz.) premium tequila blanco
- 1 tbsp agave nectar

Directions:

- Blend all the ingredients mentioned above until the required smoothness is achieved.
- Serve.

Serving: 2

Timing Information:

Preparation	Cooking	Total Time
5 min		5 min

Nutritional Information:

Calories	180 kcal
Carbohydrates	20.5 g
Cholesterol	0 mg
Fat	0.2 g
Fiber	0.7 g
Protein	0.6 g
Sodium	5 mg

* Percent Daily Values are based on a 2,000 calorie diet.

Mayan Mocha Powder

Ingredients:

- 2/3 cup nonfat dry milk powder
- 2/3 cup instant coffee granules
- 1 1/3 cups white sugar
- 1/3 cup unsweetened cocoa powder
- 1 1/2 tsps pumpkin pie spice
- 1/2 tsp ground cinnamon
- 1/4 tsp ground red pepper

Directions:

- Combine all ingredients mentioned above and put them in an airtight container.
- Serve.

NOTE: To drink just add hot water.

Serving: 12

Timing Information:

Preparation	Cooking	Total Time
5 min		5 min

Nutritional Information:

Calories	122 kcal
Carbohydrates	28.2 g
Cholesterol	1 mg
Fat	0.4 g
Fiber	0.8 g
Protein	3.1 g
Sodium	37 mg

* Percent Daily Values are based on a 2,000 calorie diet.

LICUADO DE MANGO

Ingredients:

- 1 mango, peeled, seeded and diced
- 1 1/2 cups milk
- 3 tbsps honey
- 1 cup ice cubes

Directions:

- Blend all the ingredients mentioned above until the required smoothness is achieved.
- Serve

Serving: 2

Timing Information:

Preparation	Cooking	Total Time
10 min		10 min

Nutritional Information:

Calories	255 kcal
Carbohydrates	52.1 g
Cholesterol	15 mg
Fat	3.9 g
Fiber	1.9 g
Protein	6.7 g
Sodium	82 mg

* Percent Daily Values are based on a 2,000 calorie diet.

Atole

(Spanish Hot Corn Drink)

Ingredients:

- 1/2 cup masa (corn flour)
- 5 cups water
- 1 tbsp ground cinnamon
- 5 tbsps piloncillo, brown sugar cones
- 1 tbsp vanilla extract

Directions:

- Blend masa, piloncillo, water and cinnamon in a food processor for about 3 minutes or until smooth
- Now bring this mixture to a boil over medium heat before turning down the heat to low and cooking for another five minutes.
- Remove this saucepan from heat and add vanilla.
- Pour this into mugs and serve hot.

Serving: 5

Timing Information:

Preparation	Cooking	Total Time
5 min	10 min	15 min

Nutritional Information:

Calories	68 kcal
Carbohydrates	14.1 g
Cholesterol	0 mg
Fat	0.4 g
Fiber	2.3 g
Protein	1.1 g
Sodium	8 mg

* Percent Daily Values are based on a 2,000 calorie diet.

Classical Sangrita

Ingredients:

- 1/4 cup fresh lime juice
- 1 paper-thin onion slice
- 1 cup fresh orange juice
- 1 dash Mexican-style hot sauce (such as Valentina or Cholula), or to taste
- salt to taste

Directions:

- Mix onion slice and lime juice in a medium sized bowl and let it stand as it is for about 3 hours.
- Remove onion from the juice and add salt, orange juice and hot sauce.
- Serve it cold.

Serving: 5

Timing Information:

Preparation	Cooking	Total Time
5 min		2 hr 5 min

Nutritional Information:

Calories	33 kcal
Carbohydrates	8.1 g
Cholesterol	0 mg
Fat	0.1 g
Fiber	0.2 g
Protein	0.5 g
Sodium	105 mg

* Percent Daily Values are based on a 2,000 calorie diet.

Mexican Style Ceviche

Ingredients:

- 1 (8 oz.) package imitation crabmeat, flaked
- 2 large tomatoes, chopped
- 1 red onion, finely chopped
- 1/2 bunch cilantro, chopped
- 2 limes, juiced
- 3 serrano peppers, finely chopped
- 1 tbsp olive oil
- salt and pepper to taste

Directions:

- Put shredded imitation crab in a glass bowl and mix olive oil thoroughly before adding serrano peppers, cilantro, tomato and onion.
- Pour some lime juice over the contents and add some salt and pepper according to your taste.
- Allow it to cool down for one hour before serving.

Serving: 8

Timing Information:

Preparation	Cooking	Total Time
40 min		40 min

Nutritional Information:

Calories	62 kcal
Carbohydrates	9.3 g
Cholesterol	6 mg
Fat	2 g
Fiber	1.6 g
Protein	2.9 g
Sodium	241 mg

* Percent Daily Values are based on a 2,000 calorie diet.

Mexican Green Papaya Salad

Ingredients:

Dressing:

- 1/4 cup chopped fresh cilantro, or to taste
- 3 cloves garlic, minced, or more to taste
- 2 limes, juiced
- 2 tbsps olive oil
- 1 tbsp brown sugar
- 1 pinch chili powder, or more to taste (optional)
- salt to taste

Salad:

- 1 green papaya, peeled and shredded
- 2 cups cold cooked black beans
- 1 cup cold cooked corn
- 1 red bell pepper, cut into small dice

Directions:

- Blend cilantro, garlic, olive oil, brown sugar, lime juice, chili powder and salt in a blender until the right consistency is achieved.
- Add this to a mixture of corn, papaya, red bell pepper and black beans in a large sized bowl.
- Serve.

Serving: 6

Timing Information:

Preparation	Cooking	Total Time
20 min		50 min

Nutritional Information:

Calories	168 kcal
Carbohydrates	26.9 g
Cholesterol	0 mg
Fat	5.1 g
Fiber	7.9 g
Protein	6.4 g
Sodium	313 mg

* Percent Daily Values are based on a 2,000 calorie diet.

Enchilada Sauce

Ingredients:

- 1 tbsp vegetable oil
- 1 cup diced onion
- 3 tbsps chopped garlic
- 1 tsp dried oregano
- 1 tsp ground cumin
- 1/4 tsp ground cinnamon
- 3 tbsps all-purpose flour
- 5 tbsps hot chili powder
- 4 1/2 cups chicken broth
- 1/2 (1 oz.) square semi-sweet chocolate (optional)

Directions:

- Cook onion in hot oil over medium heat in a pan until tender and add garlic, cinnamon, oregano and cumin, and cook for another two minutes.
- Now add flour and chili powder, and let the sauce get thick.
- Now add chicken broth and cook until the sauce has reached a thick state again.

- Combine chocolate and let it melt.
- Serve.

Serving: 12

Timing Information:

Preparation	Cooking	Total Time
20 min	30 min	50 min

Nutritional Information:

Calories	43 kcal
Carbohydrates	6.1 g
Cholesterol	0 mg
Fat	2.2 g
Fiber	1.7 g
Protein	1 g
Sodium	35 mg

* Percent Daily Values are based on a 2,000 calorie diet.

A Gift From Me To You...

I know you like cultural food. But what about Japanese Sushi?

Join my private mailing list of readers and get a copy of *Infinite Sushi: A*

Complete Set of Sushi and Japanese Recipes by fellow BookSumo author Hashimoto Kazuma for FREE!

Sign Me Up!

Enjoy some of the best sushi available!

You will also receive updates about all my new books when they are free. So please show your support.

Also don't forget to like and subscribe on the social networks. I love meeting my readers. Links to all my profiles are below so please click and connect :)

Facebook

Twitter

Come On...
Let's Be Friends :)

I adore my readers and love connecting with them socially. Please follow the links below so we can connect on Facebook, Twitter, and Google+.

Facebook

Twitter

I also have a blog that I regularly update for my readers so check it out below.

My Blog

ABOUT THE PUBLISHER.

BookSumo specializes in providing the best books on special topics that you care about. The *Easy Mexican Cookbook* is a collection of the best tacos and Mexican dishes available.

To find out more about BookSumo and find other books we have written go to:

http://booksumo.com/.

Can I Ask A Favour?

If you found this book interesting, or have otherwise found any benefit in it. Then may I ask that you post a review of it on Amazon? Nothing excites me more than new reviews, especially reviews which suggest new topics for writing. I do read all reviews and I always factor feedback into my newer works.

So if you are willing to take ten minutes to write what you sincerely thought about this book then please visit our Amazon page and post your opinions.

Again thank you!

INTERESTED IN OTHER EASY COOKBOOKS?

Everything is easy check out some of my other cookbooks:

Grilling:

Easy Grilling Cookbook

Smoothies:

Easy Smoothie Cookbook

Nutella

Easy Nutella Cookbook

Korean Cuisine:

Easy Korean Cookbook

Filipino Cuisine:

Easy Filipino Cookbook

Quiche:

Easy Quiche Cookbook

Burgers:

Easy Burger Cookbook

Cupcakes:

Easy Cupcake Cookbook

Printed in Great Britain
by Amazon.co.uk, Ltd.,
Marston Gate.